" The Lansdale Farmers' Market is one of the best things to happen to Lansdale. For a few hours, every Saturday, it is community day with the benefit of buying fresh fruits, vegetables, meats, bread and other items from local vendors as well as catching up with old friends and neighbors and meeting new ones. "

— Mayor Andy Szekely

Table of contents

Some of the recipes in this book reference ingredients from vendors specific to the Lansdale Farmers' Market. You may substitute any of those ingredients with your favorite brand.

Apps, Beverages & Snacks

Proud Supporter:

Carol Bailey Zellers

Longtime Lansdale resident and
patron of the Lansdale Farmers'
Market since year one.

Congratulations Lansdale Farmers'
Market on the debut of your
Market cookbook!

Saucisson en Epi
Michele Haytko

INGREDIENTS:

Freeland Market Green Peppercorn Salami

Anita's Mango Salsa

Two Sisters Blackberry Mustard

Bakers on Broad Epi Roll (or Baguette)

DIRECTIONS:

- Slice each epi roll in half or slice the baguette into 1/4 – 1/2 inch slices, and lightly toast.
- Mix together 1 teaspoon of blackberry mustard to 1 tablespoon of mango salsa.
- Slice the salami in 1/4 inch slices.
- Line as many slices of salami as desired on the toasted epi slices. Top with a teaspoon of mustard/salsa mixture. Serve at room temperature, with an additional sprinkling of fresh pepper if desired.

Dairy & Gluten Free Nachos de Huevos
Michele Haytko

INGREDIENTS:

30 Tortilla chips

4 Ironstone Creamery & Farm Chicken Eggs

1/4 cup Anita's Guacamole

1/4 cup Two Sisters Black Bean and Corn Salsa

Vegan jack cheese (optional)

DIRECTIONS:

- Arrange tortilla chips on a plate.
- Crack eggs on a hot, greased griddle over medium heat. Cook for 1 minute before fork scrambling with the salsa.
- Transfer the egg mixture onto the chips.
- Top with guacamole and graze jack cheese over top if desired.

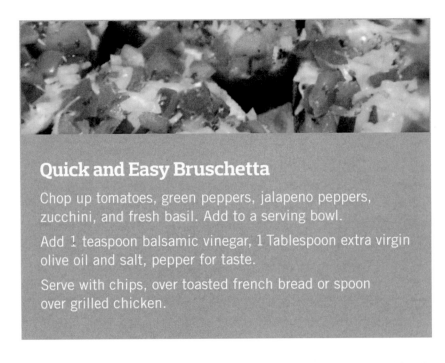

Quick and Easy Bruschetta

Chop up tomatoes, green peppers, jalapeno peppers, zucchini, and fresh basil. Add to a serving bowl.

Add 1 teaspoon balsamic vinegar, 1 Tablespoon extra virgin olive oil and salt, pepper for taste.

Serve with chips, over toasted french bread or spoon over grilled chicken.

Chocolate Coffee Brittle
Michele Haytko

INGREDIENTS:

1 ounce Joanne's Candy Kitchen Premium Wilbur
Dark Chocolate

1/4 cup Backyard Beans Punch in the Face Whole Bean Coffee

1/4 teaspoon coconut oil

DIRECTIONS:

- Melt the chocolate over low heat, stirring constantly.
  It will be thick.

- Pour the coffee beans into the chocolate, stirring well to coat.

- Lubricate a freezer safe plate with the coconut oil.
  Lay out the chocolate covered beans in a single layer.
  Freeze for 10 minutes.

- Remove from freezer and break apart. Store in the refrigerator.

Vegan, Gluten Free Chocolate Peanut Butter Balls
Michele Haytko

INGREDIENTS:

- 1 pound Nutty Novelties Peanut Butter
- 3 ounces coconut oil
- 1 tablespoon vanilla
- 2 cups powdered sugar
- 8 ounces Joanne's Candy Kitchen Dark Chocolate

DIRECTIONS:

- In a large mixing bowl, mix 2 ounces of the coconut oil with the peanut butter and vanilla.
- Slowly add in the powdered sugar and mix until smooth.
- Roll into balls and put in the freezer for 20 minutes.
- While the peanut butter balls chill, in a saucepan over low heat, melt the chocolate with the remaining coconut oil. Remove from heat.
- When the balls have chilled, dip them in the chocolate sauce, then return to the freezer for 10 minutes.
- Refrigerate until ready to serve.

Mitchell Ave Martini
Michele Haytko

INGREDIENTS (per glass):

2 ounces Boardroom Cranberry Vodka

1/2 ounce Cardinal Hollow Strawberry Wine

1/2 teaspoon World O' Honey Cranberry Honey

Fresh strawberries for garnish

DIRECTIONS:

- Shake vodka, wine, and honey together over ice. Strain and garnish with fresh strawberries.

- For best results, use the syrupy wine that is left over from boiling down strawberries in the wine for the strawberry mash in the strawberry shortcake.

St. Basil Sipper
Michele Haytko

INGREDIENTS (per glass):

1 Steep of Faith Holy Basil tea bag

6 ounces boiling water

1 tablespoon World O' Honey Cranberry Honey

2 ounces Haymaker's Little Bee (Stone and Key Cellars)

Fresh mint leaves and lemon for garnish

DIRECTIONS:

- Pour boiling water over the tea bag and steep for 4 minutes. Discard tea bag.
- Stir in honey until dissolved.
- Once the tea is room temperature, stir in the Little Bee and pour the mixture over ice. Garnish and serve with sliced lemons and fresh mint.

West Ward Julep
Michele Haytko

INGREDIENTS (per glass):

1/4 cup Haymaker's Little Bee (Stone & Key Cellars)

1/4 cup Woodford Reserve Bourbon (or your favorite bourbon)

1 teaspoon World O' Honey Cranberry Honey

10-12 fresh mint leaves (plus extra for garnish)

DIRECTIONS:

- Muddle the mint and honey together with a large mortar and pestle.

- Add the bourbon in the mortar directly, and swish gently to remove all of the mint oil.

- Strain over crushed ice as you pour in the Little Bee.

- Garnish with fresh mint.

Lansdale Sangria
Michele Haytko

INGREDIENTS (per glass):

1/4 cup Cardinal Hollow Strawberry Wine

1/4 cup Mickley's Orchard Fuji Apple Juice

1/4 cup Haymaker's Sweet Leaf (Stone & Key Cellars)

Sliced Mickley's apples and Just Kiddin Around's strawberries for garnish

DIRECTIONS:

- Shake together the three liquids and pour over ice.
- Garnish with apples and strawberries.

Soups & Salads

Proud Supporter:
Windy Springs Farm

Baked Potato Soup
Lou Supina

INGREDIENTS:

4 large baking potatoes

2/3 cup butter

2/3 cup all-purpose flour

6 cups of milk

3/4 teaspoon salt

1/2 teaspoon pepper

4 green onions, chopped and divided

12 slices of bacon, cooked, crumbled and divided

1-1/4 cups (5 ounces) shredded cheddar cheese, divided

1 (8 ounces) carton of sour cream

DIRECTIONS:

- Wash potatoes and prick several times with a fork; bake at 400 degrees for 1 hour or until done. Let cool.
- Cut potatoes in half lengthwise and scoop out pulp.
- Melt butter in a heavy saucepan over low heat; add flour, stirring until smooth.
- Cook 1 minute, stirring constantly.
- Gradually add the 6 cups of milk; cook over medium heat – stirring constantly – until mixture is thickened and bubbly.
- Add potato pulp, salt, pepper, 2 tablespoon green onions, 1/2 cup crumbled bacon, and 1 cup cheese to saucepan.
- Cook until thoroughly heated; stir in sour cream. Add extra milk if necessary, for desired consistency.

Serve with remaining bacon, onion, and cheese.

Bok Choy Salad
Tom Meyer

INGREDIENTS:

1/2 cup butter

2 tablespoon white sugar

1 ounce sesame seeds

2 pkgs ramen noodles (broken up, minus the flavor packet)

1 sm pkg slivered almonds

2 lbs. bok choy

6 green onions

DRESSING:

3/4 cup vegetable oil

1/4 cup red wine vinegar

1/2 cup white sugar

2 tablespoon soy sauce

Mix well and chill until ready to use

DIRECTIONS:

- In large skillet melt butter over medium heat.
- Add sesame seed, noodles, almonds and sugar.
- Stir continuously until lightly browned. Set this crunchy topping mixture aside to cool to room temperature.
- Coarsely chop bok choy and green onions then toss together and chill until ready to serve.
- Just before serving, break up the crunchy topping mixture, add to bok choy, pour dressing over, mix and serve.

Cucumber and Tomato Salad
Joy Petka

SALAD INGREDIENTS:

- 3 cups sliced cucumbers
- 3 roma tomatoes
- 1/3 cup chopped red onion
- 1/4 cup fresh basil

DRESSING INGREDIENTS:

- 1/4 cup extra virgin olive oil
- 3/4 cup apple cider vinegar
- 1/2 tablespoon red wine vinegar
- 1/2 teaspoon dill weed
- 1 teaspoon sugar
- 1/4 teaspoon salt
- 1/4 teaspoon pepper

DIRECTIONS:

- Mix all dressing ingredients together and drizzle over salad.

Strawberry Spinach Salad
Maryann L.

SALAD INGREDIENTS:

10 ounces baby spinach

1 pint strawberries

DRESSING INGREDIENTS:

1/2 cup vegetable oil

1/4 cup white wine vinegar

1/2 cup sugar

1 tablespoon poppy seeds

1 1/2 teaspoon minced onion

1/4 teaspoon paprika

1/4 teaspoon Worcestershire sauce

DIRECTIONS:

- Wash spinach, remove stems and dry thoroughly.
- Thinly slice strawberries.
- Combine dressing ingredients.
- Just before serving toss spinach, strawberries and dressing together.

Watermelon Salad with Mint Jelly
Two Sisters Canning

DIRECTIONS:

- Cube fresh watermelon.
- To a large bowl add the cubed watermelon, raspberries, blueberries, sliced strawberries and grapes.
- Stir in a few tablespoons of the Mint Jelly for the dressing. Top with fresh mint leaves and serve.

Orange Summer Salad

DIRECTIONS:

- Cut or tear romaine lettuce and add to a large bowl.
- Add sliced celery, mandarin orange slices and green onions.
- Stir in a few Tablespoons of Seville Orange Vinegarette for your dressing. Top with toasted almond slices.

LFM Salad
Charisse McGill

INGREDIENTS:

- 1 bag Humble Huckster salad mix
- 2 tomatoes from Just Kiddin Around farm
- 2 green or red peppers from Windy Springs Farm
- 1 cucumber from Lapinski's farm
- 1 shallot (chopped) from Kimberton CSA
- 1 bottle of World O' Honey dressing

DIRECTIONS:

- Put all ingredients in a bowl, except dressing.
- Toss to mix well.
- Drizzle with dressing and serve immediately.

Tuscan Tuna Salad
Kristina Jeyaraj

INGREDIENTS:

2 cans white solid tuna

1 can garbanzo or canelli beans drained and rinsed

1/4 cup diced celery

1/4 cup diced carrots

1/4 cup diced red onion

1/4 cup diced olives

3 tablespoons olive oil

1 tablespoon balsamic vinegar

Salt and pepper to taste

Arugula, spinach, or any greens of your choice

Crusty bread

DIRECTIONS:

- Add the tuna, beans, onion, celery, carrot, and olives together in a bowl.
- Gently toss with the olive oil and balsamic vinegar. Add salt and vinegar to taste.
- Serve over greens and with a great crusty bread!

Homemade Buttermilk Ranch Dressing

1/2 - 3/4 cup well-shaken buttermilk.

2-3 tablespoons sour cream.

1-2 tablespoons mayonnaise.

1 teaspoon finely chopped fresh tarragon, dill, parsley, chives or celery leaves (or a combination)

1 clove garlic, finely minced with a microplane grater.

1/2 teaspoon dijon mustard.

Side Dishes

Proud Supporter:

CUSTOM FRAMING AT ITS BEST

Proud Supporter:

FARMERS' MARKET
BUSINESS INCUBATOR

Roasted Asparagus with Lemon and Sea Beans
Michele Haytko

INGREDIENTS:

1 pound Farm Asparagus

1/8 pound Mainly Mushrooms Sea Beans

2 tablespoons Mediterranean Delicacies Olive Oil

1 large lemon, zested, sliced thin with edge reserved
for juicing

DIRECTIONS:

- Preheat the oven to 300 degrees.
- Trim and cut the asparagus and lay in a single layer in a baking dish.
- Clean the sea beans and layer them loosely atop the asparagus.
- Sprinkle the zest over the greens before drizzling the olive oil generously.
- Place the sliced lemon around the dish and juice the edges over the dish. Cover with foil.
- Bake for 30-40 minutes until the asparagus is tender.

INGREDIENTS:

Ingredients:

- 5 pieces Ironstone Bacon
- 1 1/2 Mickley's Orchard Apples
- 1 Kimberton Farm Red Onion, diced
- 1 pound Mickley's Brussel Sprouts, cut in half

DIRECTIONS:

- Cut 5 pieces of thick bacon in half and then dice or julienne to preference. Toss in a pan over medium heat (once hot) and cook for 5 minutes. DO NOT DRAIN.
- Add in the apples, bacon and diced onion.
- Cook for 5 minutes.
- Add in brussel sprouts.
- Cover and cook for 15-20 minutes, or until dark green and soft. Serve warm or at room temperature.

Rosemary Baked Root Vegetables
Michelina Jones

INGREDIENTS:

1 small butternut squash, cubed

4 beets

1 large onion

4 sweet potatoes, cubed

3 tablespoons extra virgin olive oil

1 garlic clove

2 tablespoons rosemary

salt and pepper to taste

1 tablespoon lemon juice

1/3 cup apple cider vinegar

DIRECTIONS:

- Sautée chopped onions for few minutes (until clear).
- Coat vegetables in olive oil and mix in vinegar, lemon juice, rosemary, salt and pepper. Spread vegetables out evenly in a cooking pan.
- Roast the vegetables at 475 degrees for 45 minutes to 1 hour or until tender and golden brown (stirring occasionally).

Baked Pineapple Bread Casserole
Mary Supina

INGREDIENTS:

1 stick butter

1/2 cup sugar

4 eggs

1 can of crushed pineapple with juice

5 slices of bread cut into cubes

DIRECTIONS:

- Grease a 1 1/2 quart casserole dish.
- Cream together butter and sugar.
- Add eggs and beat well.
- Add pineapple and juice.
- Stir in bread cubes.
- Bake at 350 degrees in the pre-greased casserole dish – uncovered for 1 hour.

Cashew Rice
Fran Supina

INGREDIENTS:

1/4 cup of butter

1/3 cup of chopped onion

1 cup of rice

2 cups of chicken broth

1/2-1 tsp of salt

1/2 cup cashews

1/4 cup of chopped parsley

DIRECTIONS:

- Melt butter in large saucepan.
- Add onion, stir until soft.
- Add rice and stir until coated.
- Stir in broth and salt then cover.
- Simmer 25-30 minutes until liquid is absorbed.
- Stir in cashews and parsley.

Chipotle Smashed Sweet Potatoes
Benny L

INGREDIENTS:

2 large sweet potatoes, peeled and cubed

2 tablespoon unsalted butter

1 adobo chipotle pepper (in canned adobo sauce) chopped

1 teaspoon adobo sauce from can of peppers

1/2 teaspoon salt

DIRECTIONS:

- Put cubed potatoes into a steamer basket and place into a large pot of simmering water.
- Allow to steam for 20 minutes or until the potatoes are fork tender.
- Add butter to potatoes and mash with potato masher.
- Add peppers, sauce, and salt. Continue mashing to combine.
- Serve hot.

Twice Baked Potatoes
Nancy Donovan Cohen

INGREDIENTS:

4 large baking potatoes

1 tablespoon dijon-style mustard

1 small onion, chopped

8 ounce yogurt

1 tablespoon butter

3 tablespoons milk, or to taste

1/2 lb fresh string beans

salt and pepper

DIRECTIONS:

- Bake potatoes at 400 degrees for 1 hour. Cool.
- Saute onion in butter until limp. Cut beans into 1 inch lengths.
- Cook until barely done – about 3 minutes. Run under cold water.
- Cut potatoes in 1/2 lengthwise and remove pulp, leaving 1/4 inch shell.
- Mash potato pulp, add mustard, yogurt and milk. When smooth, stir in beans, onion, salt and pepper.
- Mound high in potato skins and bake at 400° until warm, about 15-20 minutes.

Carrot Casserole
Rebecca Lieberman

INGREDIENTS:

2 cups cooked carrots

3 eggs or egg substitute

1/4 cup sugar

1 cup milk, full or skim

1/2 cup soft margarine or butter

1/4 teaspoon cinnamon

2 tablespoons flour

1 tablespoon baking powder

DIRECTIONS:

- Put all ingredients in blender/food processor and mix.
- Pour into greased 2-quart casserole.
- Bake, un-covered, at 350 degrees for 30-45 minutes. Done when knife inserted comes out clean.
- If making ahead of time, refrigerate and add 15 minutes to baking time. (I have sometimes poured these ingredients into a pie shell and baked.)

Green Beans
C. McCann

INGREDIENTS:

- 2 tablespoons butter
- 2 tablespoons chopped onions
- 1 tablespoon brown sugar
- 1 teaspoon Dijon mustard
- 1 teaspoon honey
- 1 1/2 lbs green beans
- 2 tablespoons almonds
- zest of lemon

DIRECTIONS:

- Sautee onions and butter until clear.
- Add remainder to skillet until green beans are to your liking.

Morgan's Herbal Zucchini
Rebecca Lieberman

DIRECTIONS:

- Shred and generously salt firm zucchini. Let stand one hour.
- Press out excess moisture.
- Saute zucchini in melted butter with chopped garlic, basil, marjoram, thyme, and tarragon to taste.
- Serve with a fresh sprig of herb for garnish.

Herbed Potatoes
Maryann L.

INGREDIENTS:

5 pounds of small potatoes, quartered

1/4 cup extra virgin olive, or avocado oil

2 tablespoon chopped fresh parsley*

1 tablespoon chopped fresh rosemary*

1 teaspoon chopped fresh thyme*

sea salt

freshly ground black pepper

can substitute dried herbs

DIRECTIONS:

- Preheat oven to 400 degrees.
- In a roasting pan or dish toss quartered potatoes with oil and herbs.
- Sprinkle with sea salt and pepper.
- Roast for 35-45 minutes, turning potatoes a few times so they brown evenly, until golden brown.

Broiled Zucchini With Parmesan

Rebecca Lieberman

INGREDIENTS:

4 zucchini, no longer than 6 inches each

2 tablespoons melted butter or olive oil

salt and pepper

1 teaspoon dried oregano

1/4 cup parmesan cheese

DIRECTIONS:

- Cut the ends off the zucchini and cut them lengthwise in 1/4 inch slices.
- Brush a baking sheet with butter or oil and place zucchini slices on it.
- Brush their tops with butter or oil and sprinkle with salt, pepper, oregano and cheese.
- Broil until zucchini is tender and cheese is browning.
- Serves 4-6.

(This recipe was in The Reporter in 1991 and I've served it many times since.)

QUICK TIP

It's easy to tell if eggs are fresh...a fresh egg will sink in water, a stale egg will float

Entrees

LIQUID MEASURES

1 gal = 4 qt = 8 pt = 16 cup = 128 fl oz.
1/2 gal = 2 qt = 4 pt = = 8 cups = 64 fl oz.
1/4 gal = 1 qt = 2 pt = 4 cups = 32 fl oz.
1/2 qt = 1 pt = 2 cups = 16 fl oz.
1/4 qt = 1/2 pt = 1 cup = 8 oz.

DRY MEASURES

1 cup = 16 tbsp = 48 tsp = 250 ml
3/4 cup = 12 tbsp = 36 tsp = 175 ml
2/3 cup = 10 2/3 tbsp = 32 tsp = 150 ml
1/2 cup = 8 tbsp = 16 tsp = 75 ml
1/3 cup = 5 1/3 tbsp = 16 tsp = 75 ml
1/4 cup = 4 tbsp = 12 tsp = 50 ml
1/8 cup = 2 tbsp = 6 tsp = 30 ml
1 tbsp = 3 tsp = 15 ml

QUICK EQUIVALENCY CHART

3 teaspoons = 1 tablespoon
2 tablespoons = 1/8 cup = 1 fl oz
4 tablespoons = 1/4 cup = 2 fl oz
5 tablespoons + 1 teaspoon = 1/3 cup
8 tablespoons = 1/2 cup
1 cup = 1/2 pint
4 cups = 2 pints = 1 quart
4 quarts = 1 gallon
16 ounces = 1 pound
Dash or pinch = less than 1/8 teaspoon

Chicken with Wild Mushroom Sauce (Serves 4)
Patty Darrah

INGREDIENTS:

4 boneless chicken breasts (pounded to 1/4 inch thickness)

1-2 shallots diced

1/4 - 1/2 lb mixed wild mushrooms, brushed and sliced (chanterelle, morel, hen of the woods)

3 tablespoons butter

1 tablespoon olive oil

salt & pepper

1/2 cup white wine

heavy cream (if desired)

DIRECTIONS:

- Melt 1 tablespoon of butter in pan over medium high heat and add oil.
- Saute the chicken breasts over medium high heat until golden brown on both sides and no longer pink in the center (3-5 min per side).
- Remove from pan and hold on covered plate.
- Reduce heat and add 2 tablespoons of butter to pan.
- Add chopped shallots and saute over medium-high heat until translucent.
- Add prepared mushrooms (brushed and sliced) to pan and sprinkle with a pinch of salt.
- Saute mushrooms until they release their juices and start to wilt.
- Remove mushrooms and shallots from pan and set aside.
- Deglaze the pan with white wine (about 1/2 cup) and let simmer until slightly reduced.
- Add heavy cream to thicken sauce, if desired.
- Add mushrooms back into sauce and pour over chicken that has been kept warm.

Joe's Green Pepper and Onion Quiche
Lou Supina

INGREDIENTS:

1 refrigerated pie crust softened as directed on box

1/2 medium-size green or red pepper finely chopped

1/2 medium-size yellow or white onion finely chopped

1 1/2 cups of shredded cheddar cheese
(monterey jack is also good)

6 eggs

1 cup of heavy cream

2 tablespoons of butter (separated)

1/2 teaspoon salt

1/2 teaspoon pepper

1/4 teaspoon garlic powder

DIRECTIONS:

- Preheat oven to 375.
- Prepare pie crust as directed on box.
- Saute green pepper and onion in 1 tablespoon of butter until translucent.
- In medium bowl, beat all remaining ingredients (excluding the butter) until well blended.
- Stir in sautéed pepper and onion.
- Pour into pie crust.
- Place 1 tablespoon of butter in the middle of the quiche.
- Bake 35-45 minutes or until knife inserted in center comes out clean. Let stand 5 minutes before serving.

(Swap out green pepper and onion for red bell pepper and ham for a tasty variation)

Pancakes or Blintzes

Lou Supina (recipe handed down from my mother)

INGREDIENTS:

2 eggs

1 tablespoon oil or butter

1 cup milk

3/4 cups of all-purpose flour

1/2 teaspoon of salt

For Cheese Filing:*

2 cups cottage cheese

1 egg yolk

sugar as you like it

1/2 teaspoon vanilla

**alternatives – blueberry pie filling, cherry pie filling,
or sliced sugared strawberries*

DIRECTIONS:

- Beat eggs, oil, and milk.
- Add flour and salt and beat until smooth.
- Refrigerate for 30 minutes until batter is like heavy cream.
  If you don't have time to refrigerate add 1 tablespoon more of
  flour in the beginning.
- Butter the pan and use medium heat – rotate pan quickly so
  batter is even in the frying pan. The pan should be hot when you
  add the batter.
- Before you turn the pancake brush it with melted butter or
  oil – then you won't have to grease the pan for the next pancake.
- The secret of good pancakes is to make it nice and thin
  without it being lacey. (Jam is better than jelly if using)

Stew (Beef Bourguignon)
Nancy Donovan Cohen

INGREDIENTS:

1 lb stew meat

Bay leaf

6 slices bacon, cooked (reserve bacon fat)

small can mushrooms, drained OR 2 ounce fresh mushrooms

1 can condensed beef bouillon

3 carrots

1 can water

1 medium onion

salt, pepper to taste

garlic salt to taste

DIRECTIONS:

- Brown stew meat in bacon fat.
- Pour off any excess fat.
- Add crumbled bacon, bouillon, water, salt, pepper, garlic salt & bay leaf.
- Simmer 1 hour. Add mushrooms, carrots and onion.
- Simmer 1 hour longer. Remove meat and vegetables.
- Thicken broth with flour if desired. Serve over noodles.

Serves: 4

Teppenyaki
Nancy Donovan Cohen

INGREDIENTS:

12 fresh or frozen large raw shrimp, shelled and deveined

cooking oil

soy ginger sauce (below)

1/2 lb. boneless beef sirloin or top round steak

hot cooked rice

1 whole medium boneless, skinless chicken breast

3-4 vegetables*, drained and patted dry

DIRECTIONS:

- Partially freeze beef and chicken; cut across the grain into bite-sized strips.

- Toss the beef and chicken separately with a little oil. Have all ingredients ready on a large platter.

- Using a wok, skillet or electric griddle, heat 2 tablespoon oil.

- Start with vegetables that take longer to cook (carrots, leek, green pepper) and end with vegetables that take less time (pea pods, bean sprouts, water chestnuts, mushrooms, green onion). Cook half of each vegetable, stir frying until crisp-tender. Add oil if needed. Transfer to platter.

- Add half the beef, chicken and shrimp to the wok, stir fry 1-3 minutes, until the meat is done and the shrimp are pink. Transfer to platter. Repeat with remainder of vegetables, then meat. Serve at once with soy-ginger sauce and hot rice.

Soy-Ginger Sauce:

- Combine 3 tablespoon soy sauce 2 tablespoon rice vinegar or white vinegar and 1/8 tsp ground ginger.

Vegetable options: 2 cups cut up Chinese cabbage or spinach, 1 cup thinly sliced carrots, 2 leeks sliced crosswise, 1 cup green pepper cut into strips, 1 cup sliced water chestnuts, 1 cup fresh mushrooms, 1 cup fresh pea pods, 1 cup fresh bean sprouts.

Sloppy Joes
Maryann L.

INGREDIENTS:

1 pound ground buffalo or beef

1 tablespoon mustard

1 tablespoon Worcestershire sauce

1 tablespoon sugar

1 tablespoon vinegar

3/4 cup ketchup

1 chili chipotle pepper (in adobo sauce), diced/chopped

(for a less spicy version omit the chili and use bell peppers)

1 shallot or very small onion

salt to taste

DIRECTIONS:

- In a bowl mix all ingredients except meat - set aside.
- Brown meat over medium/moderate heat in a large, heavy skillet, making sure to break up large clumps.
- Add the remaining mixed ingredients (from the bowl) to the skillet and stir to mix well.
- Lower heat, stir occasionally, and cook for about 40 minutes until all flavors are incorporated.
- Use your favorite bread, bun or roll to serve.

Blueberry French Toast
Michelina Jones

INGREDIENTS:

3/4 loaf french bread

6 ounces lite cream cheese (cut in small cubes)

1/2 cup frozen blueberries

4 eggs

3/4 cup milk

2 1/2 tablespoons syrup

DIRECTIONS:

- Preheat oven to 350 degrees.
- Grease 2 quart casserole dish, cut bread in cubes place in dish, sprinkle cream cheese and blueberries over bread.
- Beat eggs milk and syrup together.
- Pour over bread. Cover with plastic wrap and refrigerate for 8 hours.
- Bake 30 minutes covered then 20 minutes uncovered.

Oven Baked French Toast
Marge Bailey

INGREDIENTS:

12 slices cinnamon raisin bread

1 pint light cream

2 large eggs

1 tablespoon ground cinnamon

6 tablespoons butter

2 tablespoons firmly packed brown sugar

2 teaspoons vanilla extract

DIRECTIONS:

- Preheat oven to 350 degrees.
- In large bowl, blend all ingredients, except bread. In lightly greased 13 x 9 inch baking pan, arrange 6 bread slices in a single layer.
- Pour 1/3 of liquid mixture evenly over bread. Arrange the remaining 6 bread slices in a single layer on top of the first layer.
- Pour remaining liquid mixture evenly over bread. Press down on bread until some liquid is absorbed and bread does not float.
- Bake until center reaches 160 degrees and bread is golden brown, about 45 minutes. Serve with bacon or sausage.

Frittata with Spinach, Potatoes and Leeks
Ann Ciesielka

INGREDIENTS:

1 tsp butter

2 cups thinly sliced leeks (about 2 large leeks)

1 (10 ounce) package fresh spinach

1/3 cup fat free milk

2 tablespoons finely chopped fresh basil

1/2 teaspoon salt

1/4 teaspoon black pepper

4 large eggs

4 large egg whites

2 cups cooked red potatoes

cooking spray

1 1/2 tablespoon dry breadcrumbs

1/2 cup (2 ounces) shredded provolone cheese

DIRECTIONS:

- Preheat oven to 350.
- Melt butter in a dutch oven over medium heat. Add leeks. Saute 4 min. Add spinach. Saute 2 min. or until spinach wilts. Place mixture in a colander, pressing until barely moist.
- Combine milk, basil, salt, pepper, eggs and egg whites. Stir well with a whisk.
- Add leek mixture and potato. Pour into a 10" round ceramic baking dish or lasagna pan coated with cooking spray. Sprinkle with breadcrumbs and top with cheese. Bake at 350 for 25 min. or until center is set.
- Before serving, broil frittata for 4 min. or until golden brown.

Herbed Spare Ribs
Michele Haytko

INGREDIENTS:

1 pound Ironstone Creamery spare pork ribs

1 tablespoon coriander seed

1 tablespoon fennel seed

1 tablespoon dried marjoram

1 teaspoon onion powder

1 teaspoon garlic powder

½ teaspoon black pepper powder

2 tablespoons World O' Honey Cranberry Honey

DIRECTIONS:

- Preheat oven to 300 degrees and lightly oil or foil a baking sheet with edges (to catch the meat juices).

- In a food processor, blend the coriander, fennel, and marjoram until powdered. Stir together with the onion powder, garlic powder, and black pepper.

- Generously rub both sides of the meat with the spice rub. Drizzle the honey over the top of the ribs and rub the meat to coat well.

- Cover the ribs in foil loosely and bake for 1 hour. Uncover and broil on high for 5 minutes.

- Remove the ribs from the oven and let sit for 5 minutes before slicing.

Desserts

Proud Supporter:

Strawberry Jello Mold
Mary Supina

INGREDIENTS:

6 ounce strawberry jello

1 cup of boiling water

2 - 10 ounce packages of frozen strawberries

16.5 ounce can of crushed pineapple (drained) 3

mashed bananas

1 cup chopped walnuts

1 pint of sour cream (room temperature)

DIRECTIONS:

- Dissolve jello in water.
- Add all ingredients except sour cream.
- Put 1/2 the mixture in bowl and refrigerate for 1 1/2 hours.
- Put sour cream on top of chilled and set mixture and add remaining jello. Enjoy!

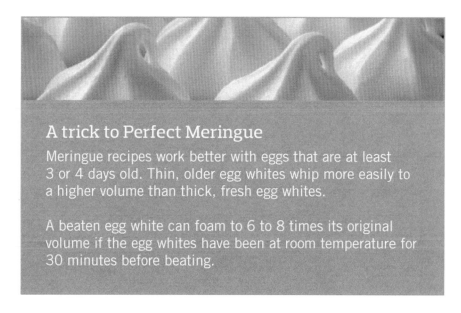

A trick to Perfect Meringue

Meringue recipes work better with eggs that are at least 3 or 4 days old. Thin, older egg whites whip more easily to a higher volume than thick, fresh egg whites.

A beaten egg white can foam to 6 to 8 times its original volume if the egg whites have been at room temperature for 30 minutes before beating.

Mom's Pumpkin Pie

Anne Scheuring

INGREDIENTS:

1 cup white sugar

1/2 teaspoon salt

1-1/2 teaspoon cinnamon

1/2 teaspoon nutmeg

1/2 teaspoon ginger

1/2 teaspoon allspice

1/2 teaspoon ground cloves

1 1/2 - 2 cups canned pumpkin

1 large can evaporated milk

2 eggs

DIRECTIONS:

- Mix all ingredients until smooth.
- Pour into shells.
- Bake at 425 degrees for 15 minutes or 350 degrees. for 50 minutes.
- Pie is done when a knife inserted in the center comes out clean.

Apple Cranberry Crumb Pie
Anne Scheuring

INGREDIENTS:

6 cups thinly sliced, peeled apples

3/4 cup sugar

3 tablespoons flour

3/4 teaspoon cinnamon

1/4 teaspoon salt

1/8 teaspoon nutmeg

1 tablespoon lemon juice

1 cup whole cranberry sauce

1 pie crust

DIRECTIONS:

- In a large bowl combine all filling ingredients; mix lightly.
- Pour into pie crust.

INGREDIENTS FOR CRUMB MIX:

1/2 cup butter

1/2 cup brown sugar

1 cup flour

- Mix well with your hands until crumbly then sprinkle over pie mixture.
- Bake at 425 degrees for 40-45 minutes.

Apple Cake with Fresh Apples
Barbara Rieck

INGREDIENTS:

1/2 cup butter, room temperature

2 cups (or 14 ounce) granulated sugar

4 eggs

1 teaspoon vanilla extract

2 cups (or 8.5 ounces) all-purpose flour

2 teaspoons baking powder

1/2 teaspoon salt

5 cups peeled & chopped apples (5-6)

1 1/2 teaspoon sugar

1 teaspoon cinnamon

DIRECTIONS:

- Grease and flour (or sugar) either a 9x13 pan or two 8x8 pans.
- Cream the butter and sugar together. Add the eggs one at a time, mixing after each addition. Add the vanilla.
- Blend the flour, baking powder and salt together and then add to the wet ingredients.
- Peel and chop the apples and stir into the batter.
  Place in prepared pan(s).
- Combine the cinnamon and sugar and sprinkle on top of batter.
- Bake at 350 degrees for 45 minutes (for either 1 or 2 pans) until a toothpick inserted in the center of the pan(s) comes out clean. Let cool.

Pretty easy recipe that freezes well. Uses apples, butter, eggs and cinnamon available from the Farmers' Market!

Blueberry Oatmeal Muffins
Michelina Jones

INGREDIENTS:

- 1 cup quick oats
- 1 1/4 cup all-purpose flour
- 1/2 cup brown sugar
- 1 tablespoon baking powder
- 1/2 teaspoon baking soda
- 1/4 teaspoon salt
- 1 cup greek yogurt
- 1 large egg
- 2 teaspoons pure vanilla extract
- 1/4 cup vegetable oil
- 1 cup blueberries, rinsed and drained

DIRECTIONS:

- Combine all the dry ingredients together.
- Mix in yogurt, egg, and oil (just mix until dry ingredients are moistened)
- Fold in blueberries.
- Fill greased muffin cups 2/3 full with batter.
- Bake at 425 degrees for 20 to 25 minutes

Dairy Free Pistachio Ice Cream
Michele Haytko

INGREDIENTS:

1 can (13.5 ounce) full fat coconut milk

1 cup cashew nut milk

1/2 cup World O' Honey Cranberry Honey

4 ounces Nutty Novelties Pistachio Butter

1/2 teaspoon arrowroot powder

1/4 teaspoon salt

(Ice Cream Maker: I use an electric, non-rock salt model that requires the ice cream mixing bowl to be frozen 24+ hours. Each unit is different, so freeze your bowl or utilize rock salt as your device requires.)

DIRECTIONS:

- Mix together the ingredients in a blender or food processor for 1-2 minutes or until smooth.
- Transfer into a bowl (preferably metal) and chill for at least 2 hours.
- Pour the chilled mixture into your machine and churn as directed. Most makers make a soft serve ice cream. For more traditional, hard ice cream, transfer your churned ice cream into a freezer safe dish and freeze for 6 or more hours. If ice cream is too hard to scoop, leave at room temperature.

Banana Bread
Nancy H.

INGREDIENTS:

In larger bowl combine the following:

3 large bananas (mashed)

1 cup sugar

1 egg

1/2 stick of butter (melted)

In small bowl combine the following:

1 1/2 cups flour

1 teaspoon baking soda

1 teaspoon salt

DIRECTIONS:

- Mix dry ingredients with the wet and pour into greased/ floured bread pan.
- Bake at 325 degrees for 45-60 minutes until cooked in the center.

Almond Butter–Quinoa Blondies
submitted by Caleb Mangum (From EatingWell.com)

INGREDIENTS:

1/4 cup unsalted butter, softened

3/4 cup smooth or crunchy natural almond butter

2 large eggs

3/4 cup packed light brown sugar

1 teaspoon vanilla extract

3/4 cup quinoa flour

1 teaspoon baking powder

1/4 teaspoon salt

1 cup semisweet chocolate chips

DIRECTIONS:

- Preheat oven to 350 degrees.
- Line an 8-inch-square baking pan with parchment paper (or foil), allowing it to slightly overhang opposite ends. Coat with cooking spray.
- Beat butter and almond butter in a mixing bowl with an electric mixer until creamy.
- Beat in eggs, brown sugar and vanilla.
- Whisk quinoa flour, baking powder and salt in a small bowl.
- Mix the flour mixture into the wet ingredients until just combined. Stir in chocolate chips. Spread the batter evenly into the prepared pan.
- Bake until a toothpick inserted into the center comes out with just a few moist crumbs on it, 25 to 35 minutes. Do not overbake.
- Let cool in the pan for 45 minutes. Using the parchment (or foil), lift the whole panful out and transfer to a cutting board. Cut into 24 squares. Let cool completely before storing.

Mint Chocolate Brownies
Bobbie McKenzie

BOTTOM LAYER

1 cup sugar

1/2 cup butter

4 eggs, beat by hand before adding to mixture

1 cup flour

1/2 teaspoon salt

1 teaspoon vanilla

1 can (16 ounces) Hershey's chocolate syrup

- Mix the above ingredients and bake in 13x9 greased pan at 350 degrees for about 25 minutes.
- Cool cake before spreading the middle layer on top.

MIDDLE LAYER

2 cups powdered sugar

1/2 cup butter

3 tablespoons (or more) Creme de Menthe syrup

- Cream the butter.
- Add sugar, a little bit at a time, then add syrup.
- Mix until blended (will be thick).
- Spread on cooled cake.

TOP LAYER

1 cup chocolate chips

6 tablespoons butter

- Put butter in small pan and melt on low.
- Then add chocolate chips and melt in.
- Spread on top of cake (will be very spreadable, should not be stiff).
- Cool and cut into brownie-sized pieces.

Dye Free Red Velvet Cake
Michele Haytko

INGREDIENTS:

6 beets (Lapinski Farm)

1/2 cup water

1/3 cup lemon juice

1 tablespoon white vinegar

2 cups all-purpose flour

1 tablespoon baking powder

1 teaspoon salt

1/4 cup non-alkaline dark cocoa

6 ounces plain greek yogurt

1 tablespoon vanilla

3 eggs (Ironstone Creamery & Farm)

1 cup softened butter

1 cup cold cream cheese

4 cups powdered sugar

1/2-3/4 cup milk

DIRECTIONS:

- Roast the well-washed, skin on, and diced beets in 1/2 cup of water at 350 degrees for 90 minutes. Cool for two hours, then blend with lemon juice and vinegar until smooth.

- In a stand mixer, combine flour, baking powder, salt, and cocoa. In a measuring cup, combine yogurt, vanilla, eggs, and beet puree. Slowly add the liquids while on low, then mix at medium for 2 minutes.

- Pour into three 8" well-greased rounds, and bake at 350 degrees for 15-18 minutes or until done. Cool for 10 minutes, then remove from pans to cool fully.

- As the cake cools, prepare the frosting by whipping the butter and cream cheese until doubled in volume.

- Slowly alternate the powdered sugar and milk, adding enough milk to make the correct texture.

- When the cakes are completely cooled, frost and serve.

Simple Gluten and Dairy Free Strawberry Shortcake
Michele Haytko

INGREDIENTS:

1 package gluten free vanilla cake mix

3 Ironstone Creamery & Farm chicken eggs

1/4 cup Mediterranean Delicacies Cold Pressed, unfiltered olive oil

1/4 cup Mickley's Orchard Honeycrisp apple sauce

1 pound Just Kiddin Around strawberries (cleaned & divided into two 1/2 pound bowls)

1/2 cup plus 1 cup Cardinal Hollow Strawberry Wine

1/4 cup World O' Honey Cranberry Honey

1 ounce Joanne's Candy Kitchen Premium Wilbur Dark Chocolate

DIRECTIONS:

- Whip the eggs on medium for 2 minutes.
- Slowly add the olive oil and the apple sauce, until the eggs are doubled in volume.
- Turn the mixer to low, and add the bag of flour and the wine, mixing until well combined.
- Bake at 350 degrees, in a well greased loaf or bundt pan for 50 minutes or until the cake is done.
- While the cake is baking, heat 1/2 pound of the strawberries in 1 cup of wine over medium heat. When the wine begins to boil and the strawberries are flavorful, stir in the honey and turn to low. Simmer for 20 minutes. Remove the strawberries and mash.
- Pour 1/4 cup of the hot wine over the chocolate, whisking into syrup.
- Slice the cooled cake and place one slice on a plate, topped with the strawberry mash, another slice of cake, and some of the fresh strawberries. Drizzle the warm syrup over top.

Magic Cake
Joel Pierre Perez

INGREDIENTS:
150 grams powdered sugar

110 grams all-purpose flour or 90 grams of corn starch or potato flour

125 grams butter

1 tablespoon water

4 eggs

60 grams of good quality powdered chocolate

60 grams of coconut

50 cl of milk (dairy free milk may be used)

A pinch of salt

DIRECTIONS:
- Use a mold/pan 22 cm in diameter (8 1/2 inch).
- Preheat oven to 325 F.
- Melt butter in microwave.
- Clarify eggs (separate whites from yolks).
- Beat the egg whites with a pinch of salt until stiff.
- Blanch the yolks with sugar.
- Incorporate in order: melted butter, flour, tablespoon water.
- Stir the chocolate into milk - can be heated but do not boil.
- Finally, add the grated coconut.
- Then integrate the beaten egg whites, without crushing them, in order to obtain a fairly liquid cream with lumps.
- Pour into mold/pan and bake according to temps below.
- Conventional oven - 40 minutes
  Convection oven - 35 minutes

PROUD SUPPORTER:

We would like to thank the volunteers who donated their time and talents to make this book possible.

Michelina Jones

Maryann Law

Ted Lis

LANSDALE FARMERS' MARKET BOARD:

Tom Allebach – *President*

Carol Bailey Zellers – *Treasurer*

Charisse McGill – *Market Manager*

VENDOR REPRESENTATIVES:

Josh Davis – Freeland Market

Joe Albano – *Ironstone Creamery & Farm*

When we share recipes, the food we love, a human connection is formed. It's a unique experience; something personal. Often there is a story behind the recipe... how it was discovered, how it is a part of family lore, what makes it special in our lives.

Perhaps this Lansdale Farmers' Recipe Book is unique, because it connects those closest to the land, those with an intimate connection to creating food experiences, to a broader community that cares deeply about food. We thank all the growers, food artisans and members of the Market community for making this possible.

Share and enjoy!
Tom Allebach

Made in the USA
Middletown, DE
17 November 2017